Cover: Detail of Plate 18
A Dash for the Timber
Amon Carter Museum

Title Page: Detail of Plate 31
Self-Portrait on a Horse
Sid Richardson Collection of Western Art

FREDERIC

Remington

Paintings and Sculpture

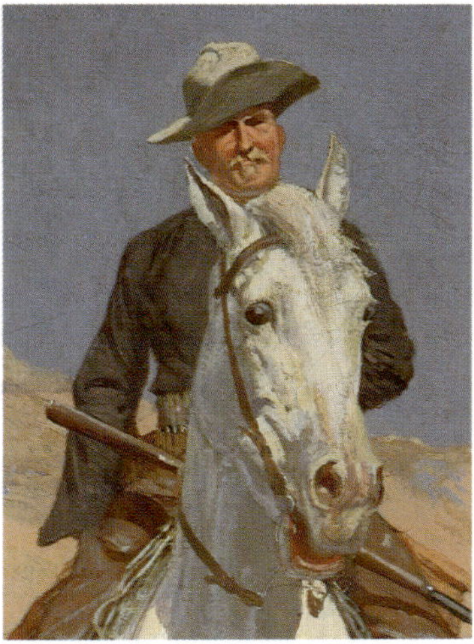

LEOPARD

This edition published in 1995 by Leopard Books
Random House, 20 Vauxhall Bridge Road, London SW1V 2SA

ISBN 0 7529 0021 8
Printed and bound in Portugal by
Printer Portuguesa Lda

"Everything in the West is life, and you want life in art... the field to me is almost inexhaustible."[1]

—*Frederic Remington*

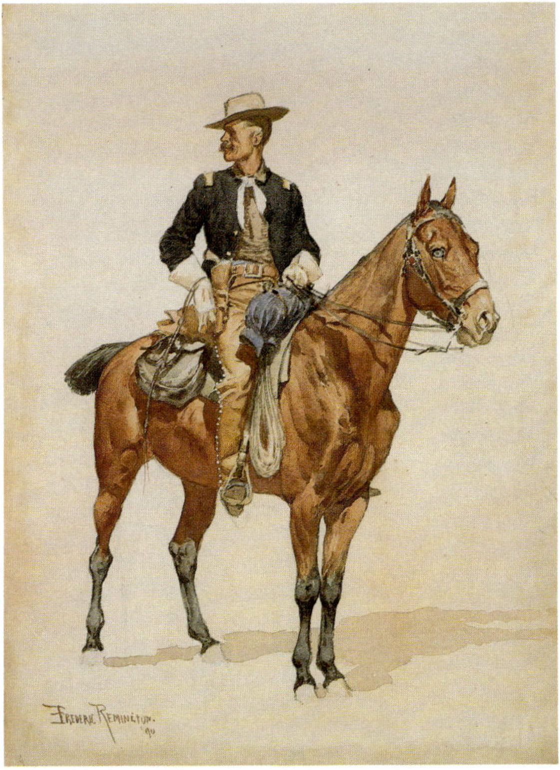

1. *Lieutenant S.C. Robertson, Chief of the Crow Scouts*

Watercolor, opaque white and graphite on paper, 1890
Amon Carter Museum

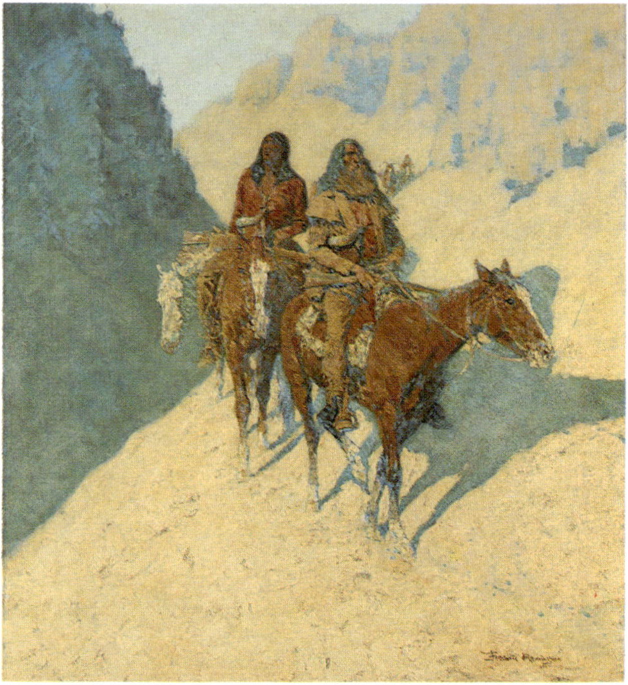

2. *The Unknown Explorers*

Oil on canvas, 1908
Sid Richardson Collection of Western Art

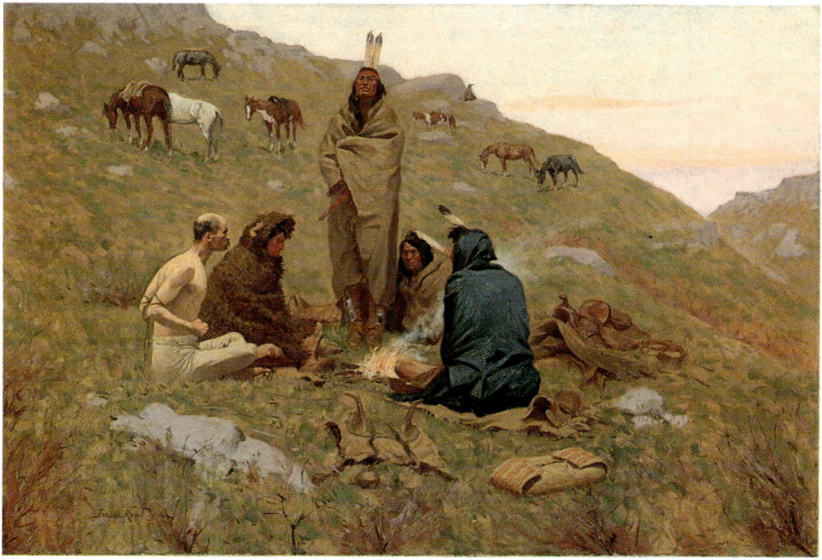

3. *Captured*

Oil on canvas, 1899
Sid Richardson Collection of Western Art

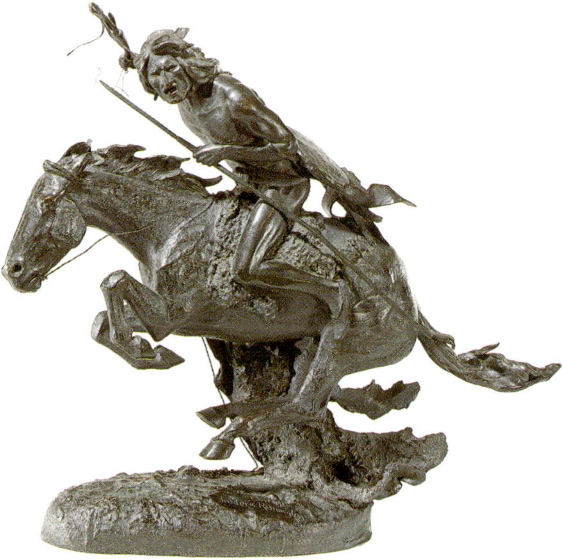

4. *The Cheyenne*

Bronze, 1907
Amon Carter Museum

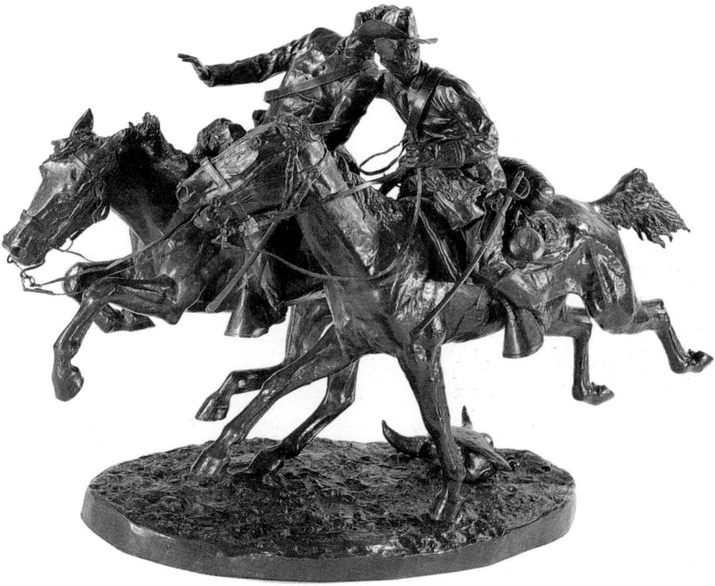

5. *Wounded Bunkie*

Bronze, 1896, cast 1899
Amon Carter Museum

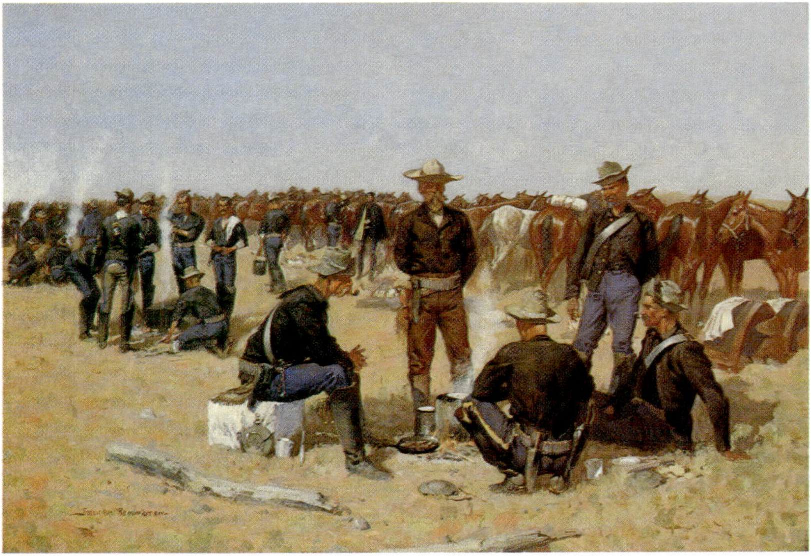

6. *A Cavalryman's Breakfast on the Plains*

Oil on canvas, c. 1892
Amon Carter Museum

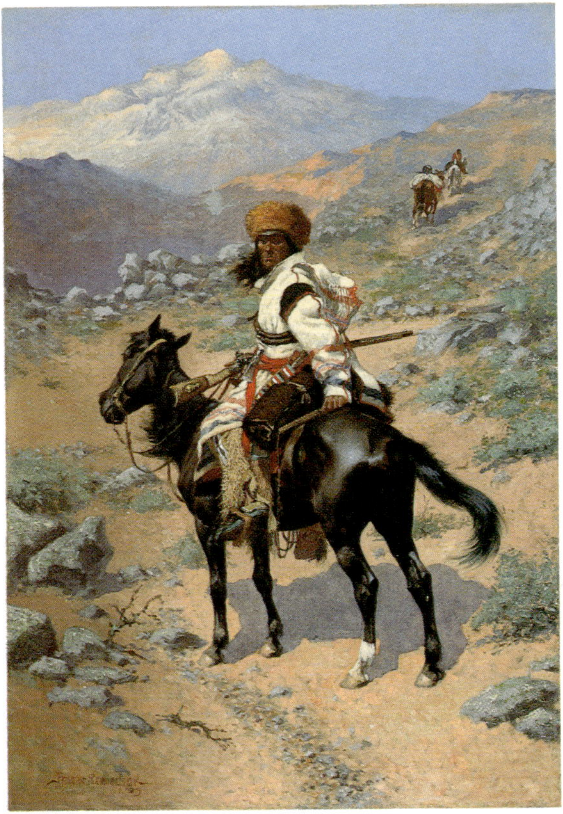

7. *An Indian Trapper*

Oil on canvas, 1889
Amon Carter Museum

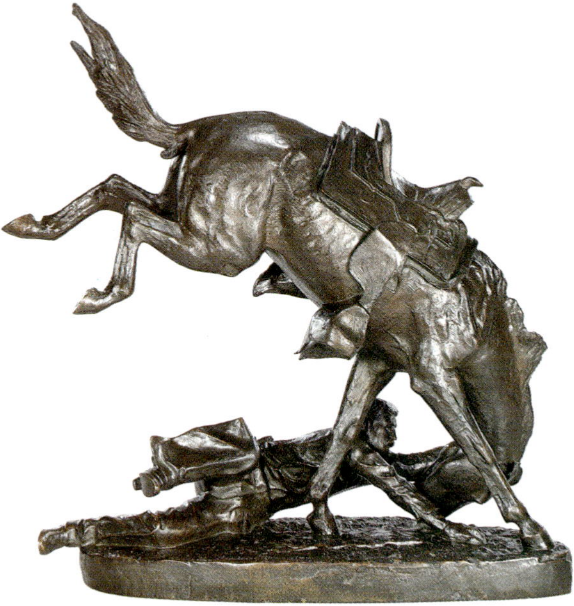

8. *The Wicked Pony*

Bronze, 1898, cast 1898
Amon Carter Museum

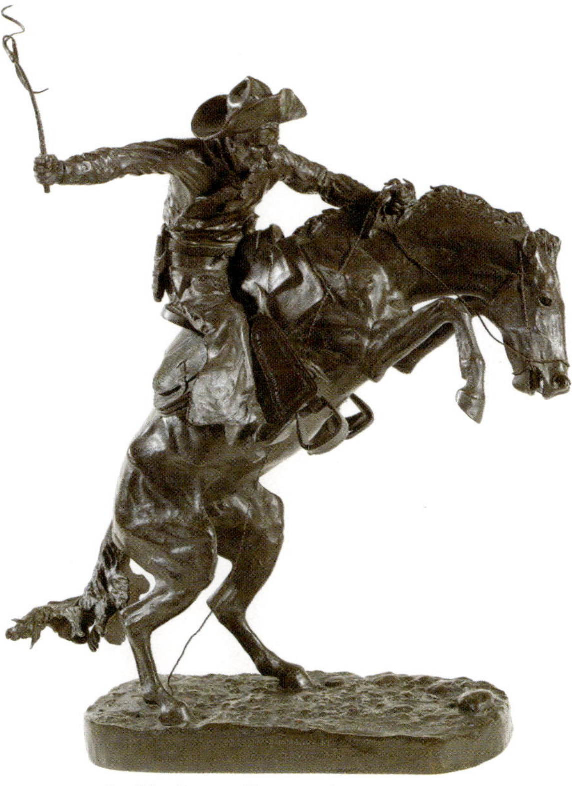

9. *The Bronco Buster*

Bronze, 1895, cast 1895
Amon Carter Museum

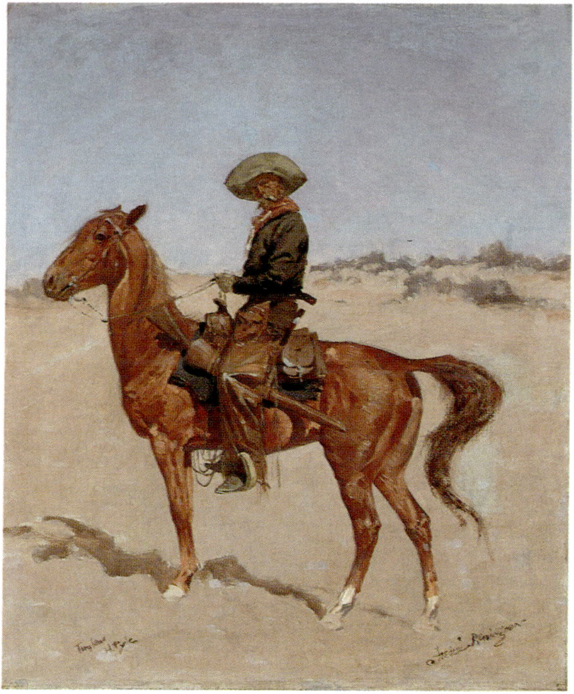

10. *The Puncher*

Oil on canvas, 1895
Sid Richardson Collection of Western Art

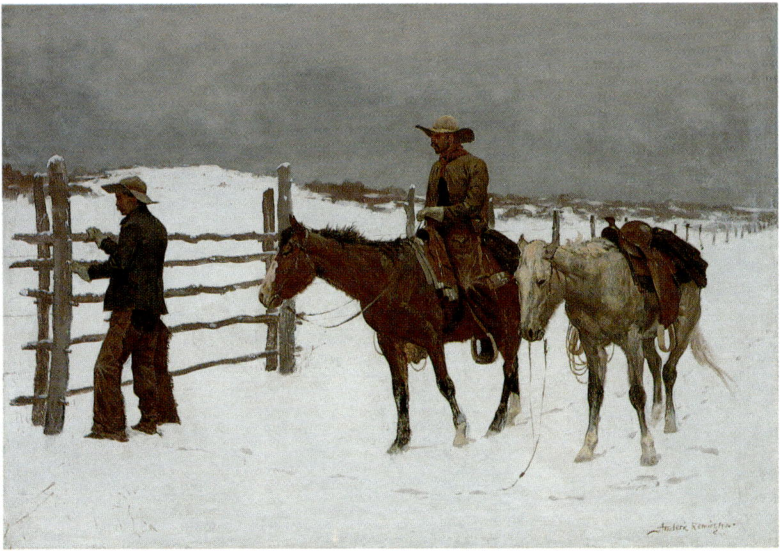

11. *The Fall of the Cowboy*

Oil on canvas, 1895
Amon Carter Museum

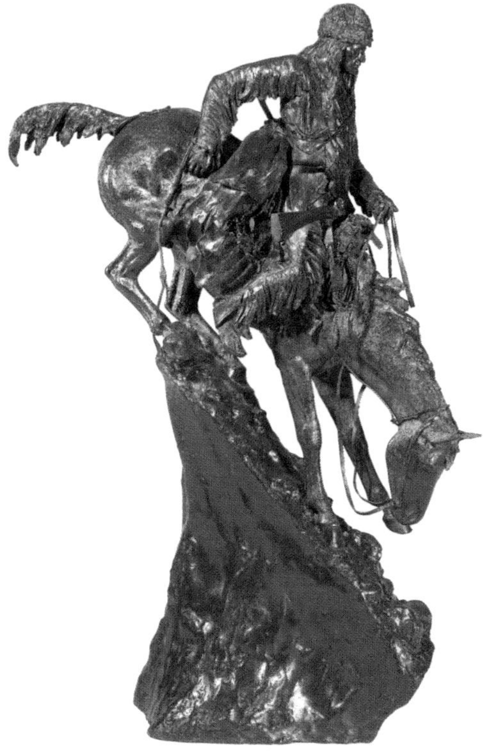

12. *The Mountain Man*

Bronze, 1903, cast c. 1914-1918
Amon Carter Museum

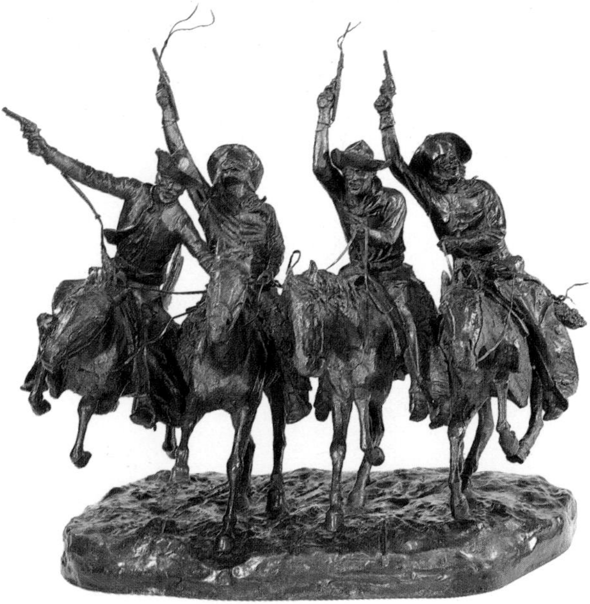

13. *Coming Through the Rye*

Bronze, 1902, cast 1916
Amon Carter Museum

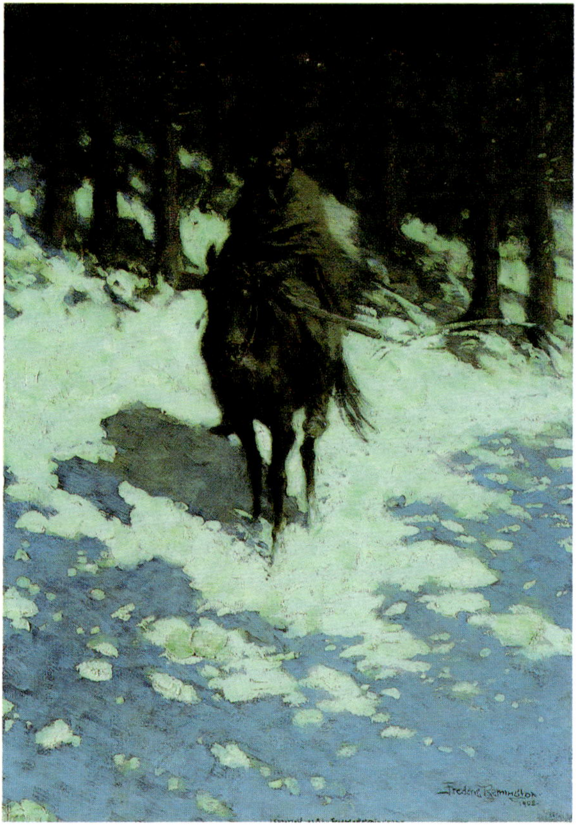

14. *A Figure of the Night (The Sentinel)*

Oil on canvas, 1908
Sid Richardson Collection of Western Art

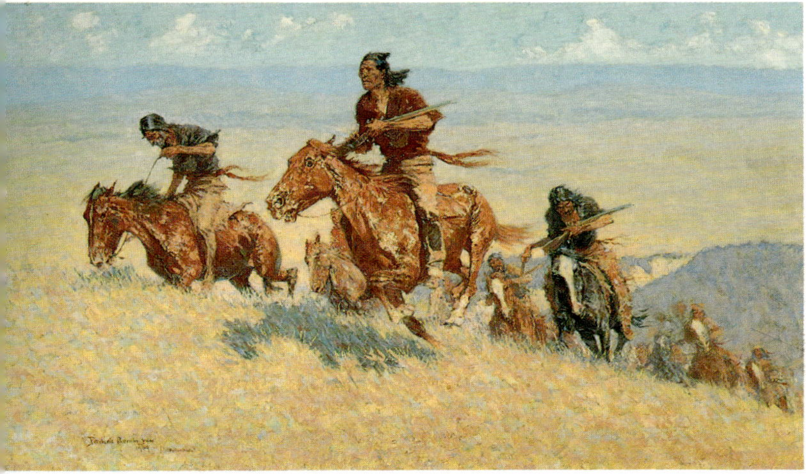

15. *Buffalo Runners, Big Horn Basin*

Oil on canvas, 1909
Sid Richardson Collection of Western Art

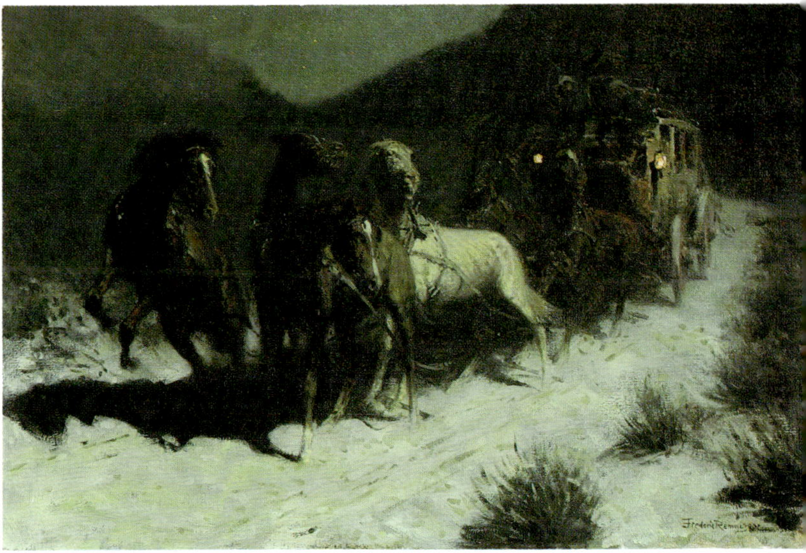

16. *A Taint on the Wind*

Oil on canvas, 1906
Sid Richardson Collection of Western Art

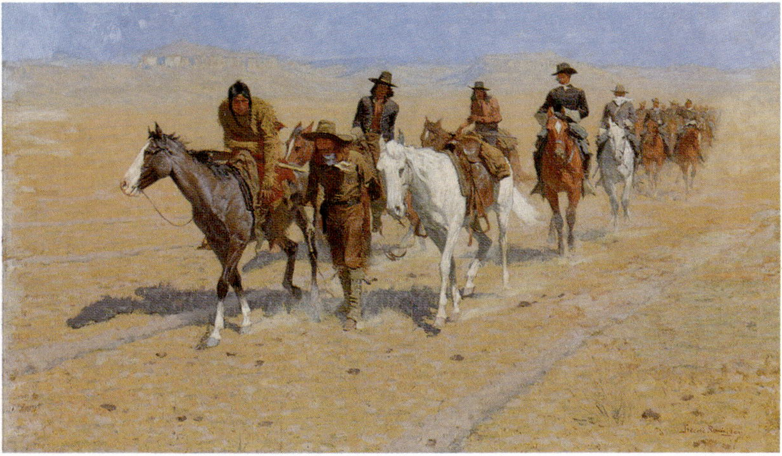

17. *Pony Tracks in the Buffalo Trails*

Oil on canvas, 1904
Amon Carter Museum

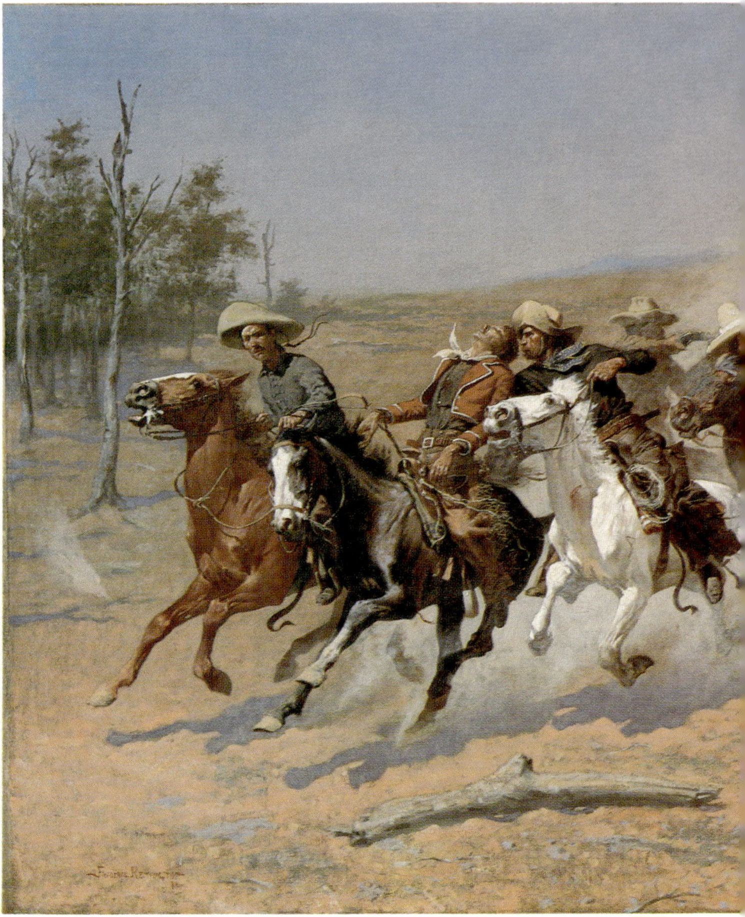

18. *A Dash for the Timber*

Oil on canvas, 1889
Amon Carter Museum

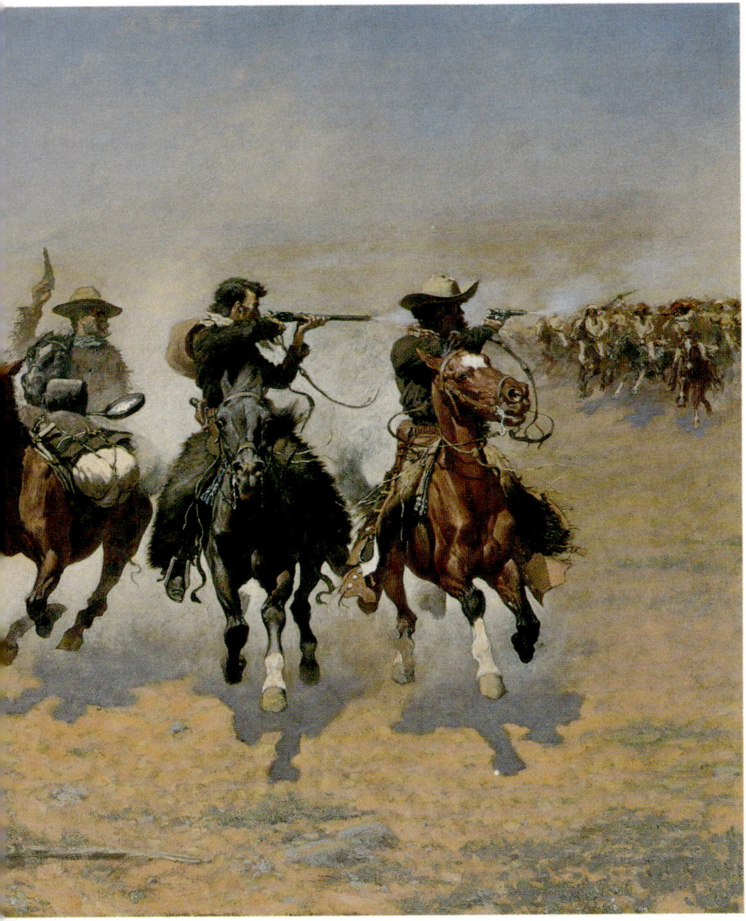

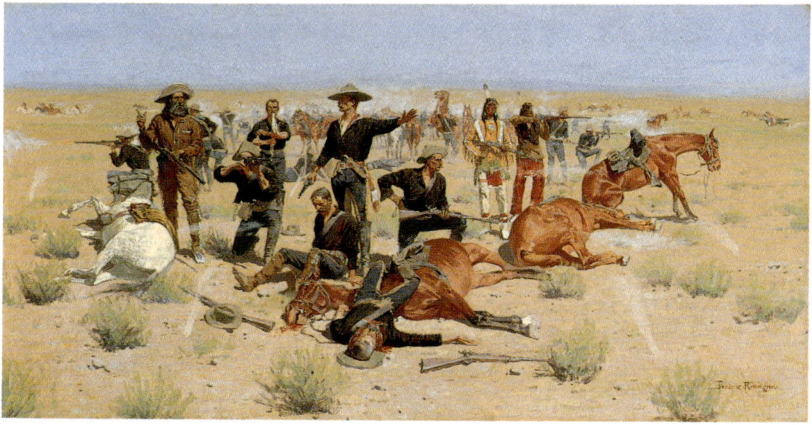

19. *Rounded–Up*

Oil on canvas, 1901
Sid Richardson Collection of Western Art

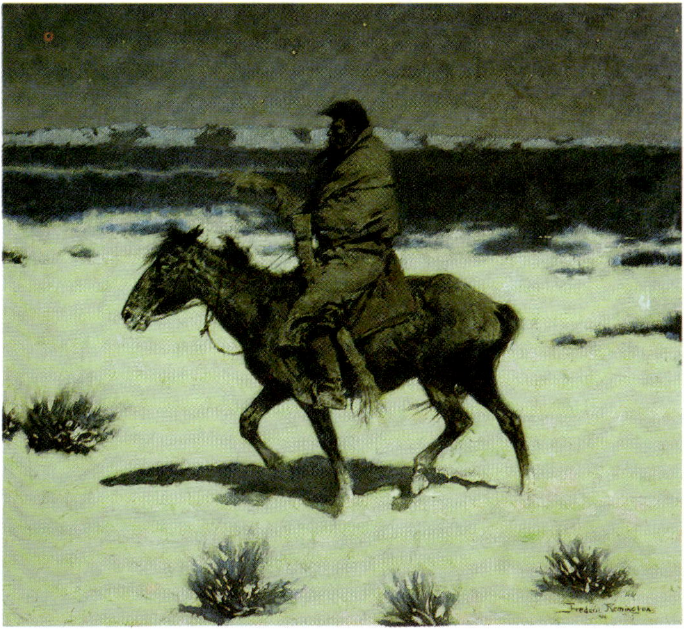

20. *The Luckless Hunter*

Oil on canvas, 1909
Sid Richardson Collection of Western Art

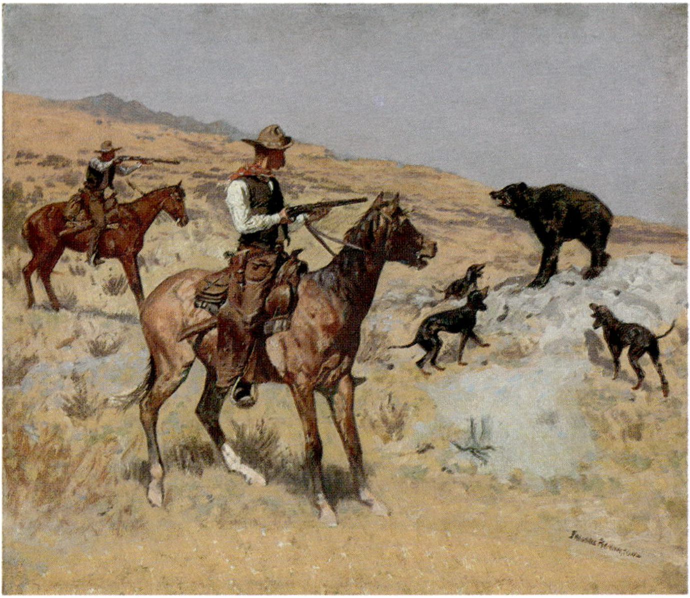

21. *His Last Stand*

Oil on canvas, 1890
Sid Richardson Collection of Western Art

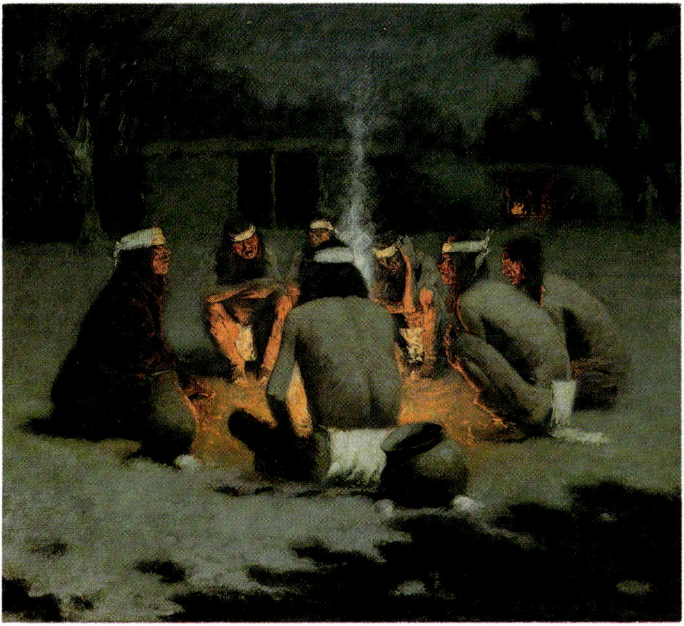

22. *Apache Medicine Song*

Oil on canvas, 1908
Sid Richardson Collection of Western Art

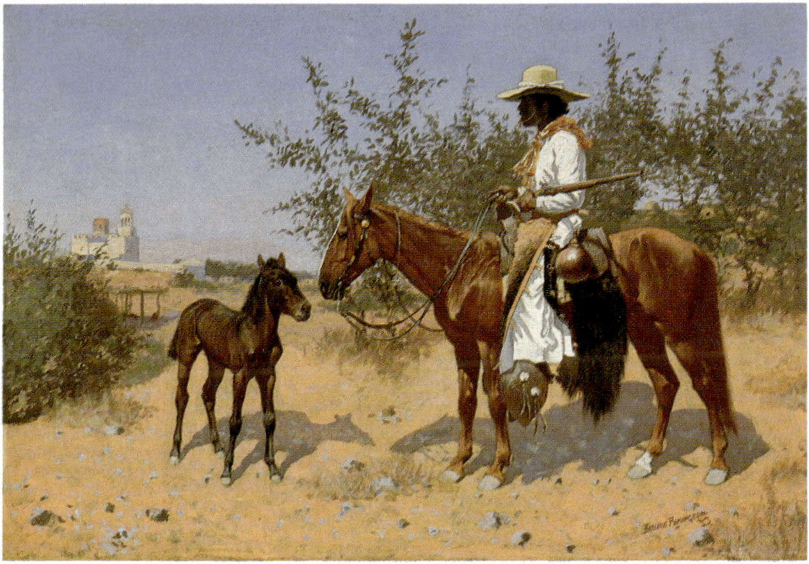

23. *The Sentinel*

Oil on canvas, 1889
Sid Richardson Collection of Western Art

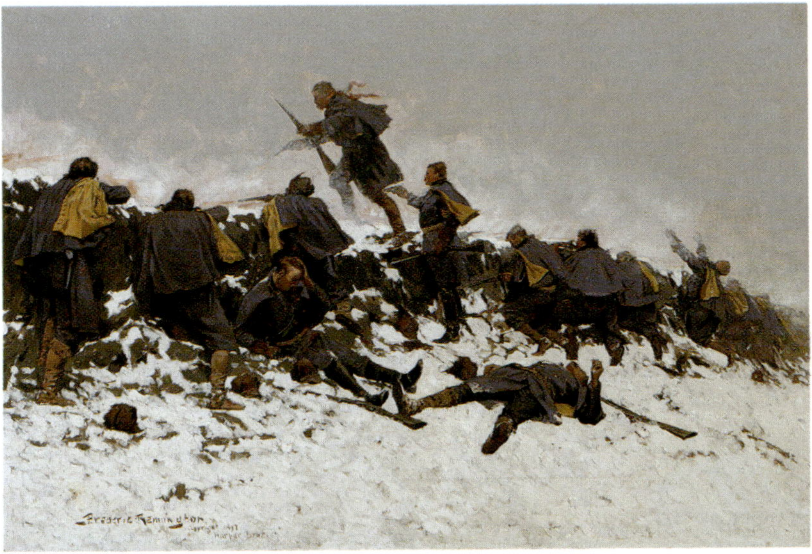

24. *Through the Smoke Sprang the Daring Soldier*

Oil on canvas, 1897
Amon Carter Museum

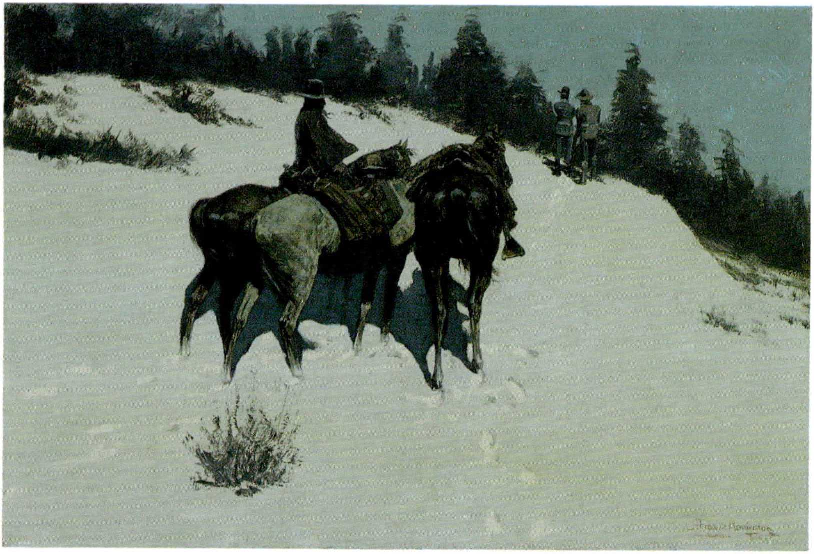

25. *A Reconnaissance*

Oil on canvas, 1902
Amon Carter Museum

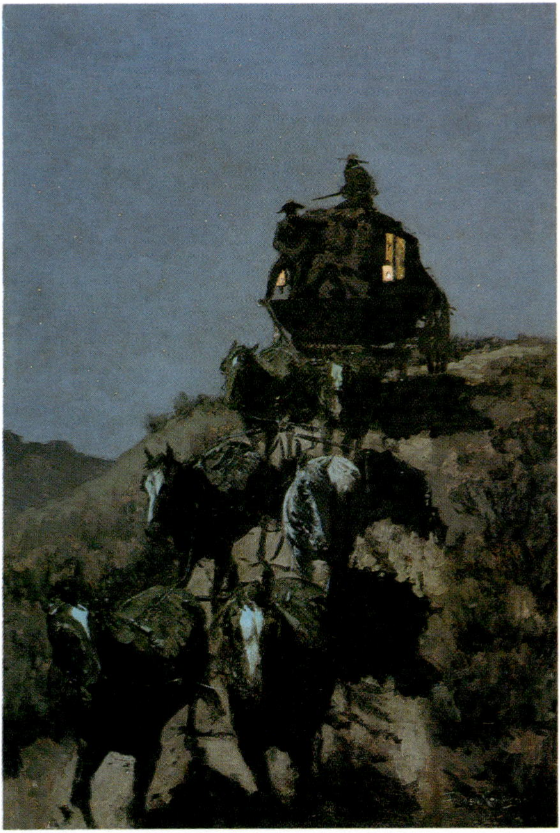

26. *The Old Stage Coach of the Plains*

Oil on canvas, 1901
Amon Carter Museum

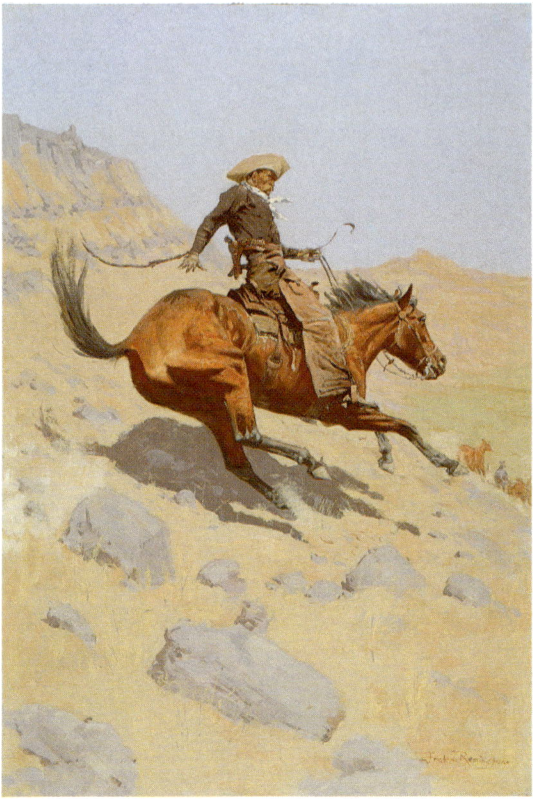

27. *The Cowboy*

Oil on canvas, 1902
Amon Carter Museum

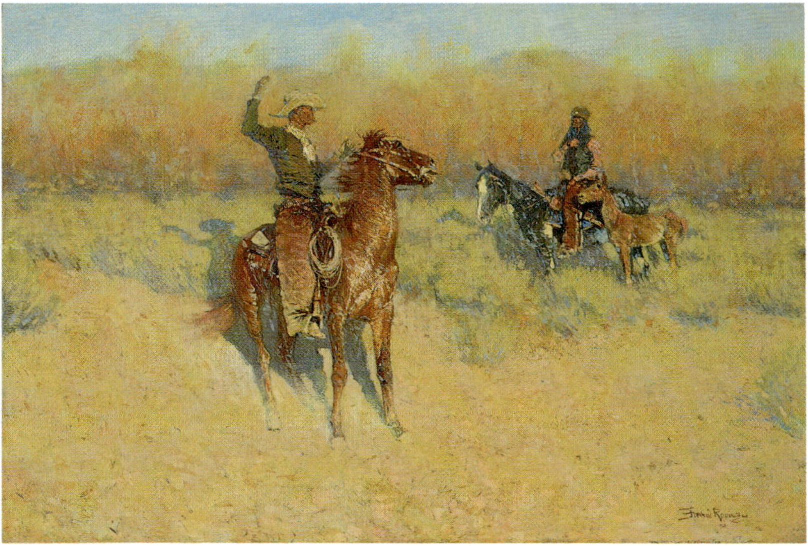

28. *The Long–Horn Cattle Sign*

Oil on canvas, 1908
Amon Carter Museum

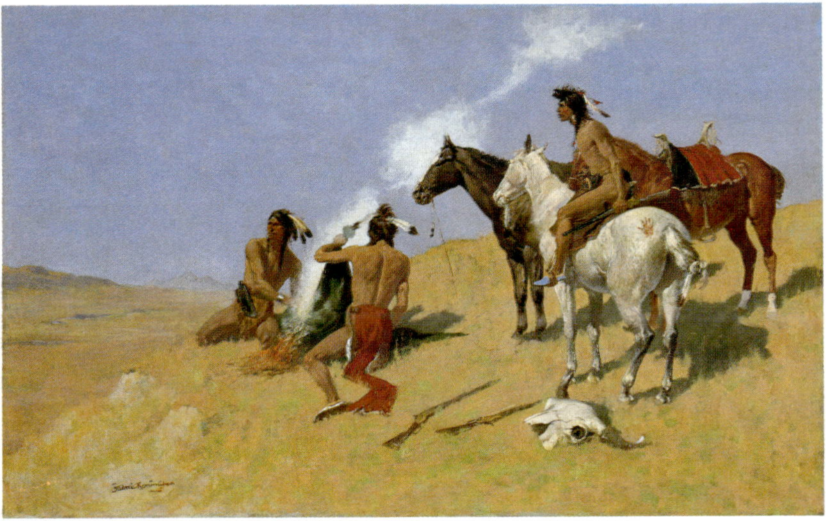

29. *The Smoke Signal*

Oil on canvas, 1909
Amon Carter Museum

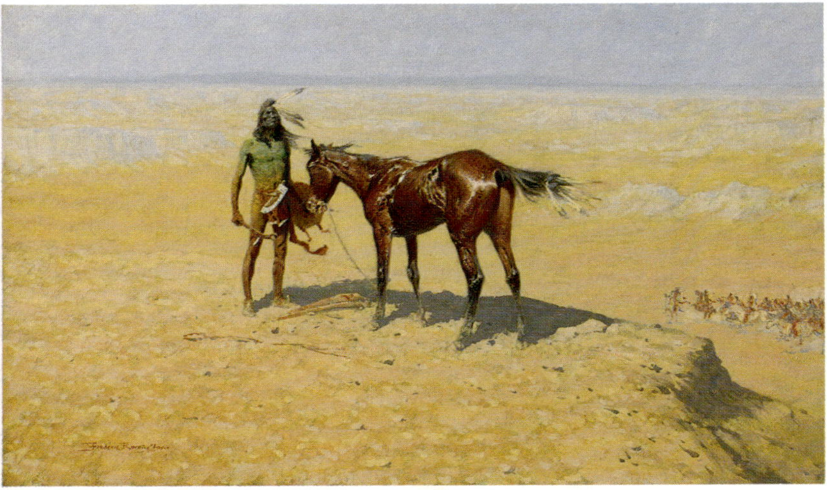

30. *Ridden Down*

Oil on canvas, 1905
Amon Carter Museum

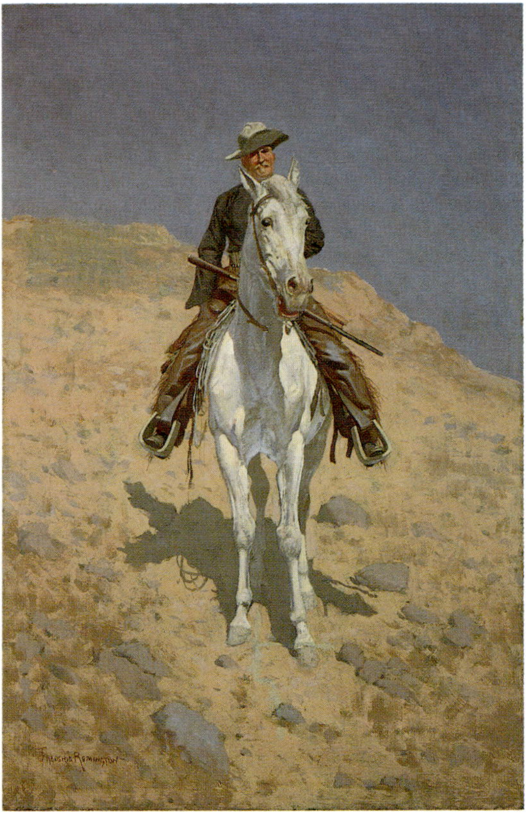

31. *Self–Portrait on a Horse*

Oil on canvas, c. 1890
Sid Richardson Collection of Western Art

Afterword

No artist or writer is more identified with the American West, its myths and its reality, than Frederic Remington. Born in upstate New York in 1841, Remington first took up drawing as an adolescent, sketching fellow cadets at the Highland Academy; as a student at the Yale School of Fine Arts, he published several drawings in the *Yale Courant*. Although family crises forced Remington to leave school and work as a clerk, art continued to consume his interest and his energies. Bored and restless at his job, Remington embarked in 1881 on a trip to the West—an area he had long wanted to explore. His imagination was totally engaged and his pen was kept busy during his few months' stay.

Upon Remington's return to the East, one of his sketches was published in *Harper's Weekly*—the start of Remington's long association with the magazine. By early 1883, the lure of the West again proved irresistible. Encouraged by a friend, Remington took up sheep ranching in Kansas and several years later became part-owner of a saloon in Kansas City. Though both endeavors lasted only a short time, they confirmed Remington's devotion to the western style of life.

In 1885, Remington settled in Brooklyn, taking art courses and selling his sketches to magazines. An assignment for *Harper's Weekly* sent him to Colorado, New Mexico, Arizona, and across the border into Mexico. The trip opened his eyes to the rugged, unforgiving landscape and the rough, hardy men who inhabited it, and inspired many paintings, including *The Sentinel* (plate 23), a stark portrait of a Papago Indian guarding a mission from the Apaches. After viewing the portfolio Remington produced on this journey, the editor of *Outing* enthusiastically declared, "Here was the real thing, the unspoiled native genius dealing with Mexican ponies, cowboys, cactus, lariats and sombreros.... No stage heroes these...."[2] Even more significant was the attention Remington attracted from Theodore Roosevelt; in 1888 Roosevelt asked *Century Magazine* to have Remington illustrate his articles on life in the West.

Remington's pursuit of recognition, both critical and financial, developed along with his technical expertise. While continuing to create pen-and-ink illustrations, Remington expanded his range of expression in watercolor paintings; in 1887 his works were included in major exhibits at the National Academy of Design and the American Water Color Society. As Remington had hoped, the exhibitions brought him not only praise but commissions from several magazines.

With camera and sketchbook in hand, Remington set out once again for the West. The hundreds of sketches, photographs, and diary entries he made during an extended trip in 1888 provided materials for both articles and illustrations. By the end of the decade, Remington had become one of America's foremost illustrators. He not only contributed to periodicals—*Fall of the*

Cowboy (plate 11) accompanied a series by Owen Wister published in *Harper's Monthly*—but illustrated books by Theodore Roosevelt, Elizabeth B. Custer, and many others. In the public's mind, he emerged as the great chronicler of the frontier, his name inextricably tied to the West.

"Remington always paints and draws the truth," wrote Julian Ralph in 1895, noting that technical difficulties sometimes made recording reality a difficult task—"The sun...is the despair of the painter as it colors the minarets of the Bad Lands."[3] Remington's primary interest, however, lay in reproducing figures rather than landscape, and his representations of Indians, cowboys, soldiers, horses, and other denizens of the West are unmatched in American art. A stickler for accuracy, Remington filled his studio with authentic Indian and cowboy paraphernalia to use for reference as he worked; his desire to portray action as realistically as possible was equally pressing. That he achieved both is undeniable. In *An Indian Trapper* (plate 7), for example, Blackfoot dress, weapons, implements, and modes of decoration are represented with meticulous care.[4] And the action-packed *A Dash for the Timber* (plate 18), first exhibited at the National Academy of Design in 1889, drew accolades from the *New York Herald*:

> This work marks an advance on the part of one of the strongest of our younger artists. The drawing is true and strong, the figures of the men and horses are in fine action, tearing along at full gallop....[5]

Despite his declared objectivity, elements of mystery and romantic imagery are certainly present in Remington's paintings. The enigmatic quality seen in the faces of his Indians no doubt stemmed from his feeling that "No white man can ever penetrate the mystery of their minds or explain the reasons of their acts."[6] His approach to soldiers and cowboys, in contrast, is solidly empathetic; his growing identification with these independent, self-reliant men can be seen in *Self-Portrait on a Horse* (plate 31), a work which embodied his belief that cowboys "possess a quality of sturdy, sterling manhood which would be to the credit of men in any walk of life."[7] Working these figures into his narrative paintings, Remington betrayed both his prejudices and his utter immersion in the codes of the White Man's West. For Remington, the West was a great battleground—man against nature, cowboy against Indian, civilization against savagery. In both *Captured* (plate 3) and *Rounded Up* (plate 19), the soldiers exhibit remarkable grace under pressure, remaining calm and stoical despite the presence of hostile Indians and the near-certainty of death, while paintings like *Pony Tracks in the Buffalo Trails* (plate 17) "celebrate the everyday gallantry and courage of the frontier regulars and the professional officers who led them."[8] These became the icons the public treasured, for as William Coffin noted in 1892, "Eastern people have formed their conceptions of what the Far-Western life is like more from what they have seen in Mr. Remington's pictures than from any other source."[9]

Critics and the public were taken, too, by Remington's sculptures, an art form the artist embraced because, as he wrote, "My oils...will look like pale molases [sic] in time—my water colors will fade—but I am to endure in bronze...."[10] The excitement and action inherent in his paintings leapt to life in such works as *The Bronco Buster* (plate 9), *The Wicked Pony* (plate 8) and *The Wounded Bunkie* (plate 5).

New casting methods introduced at the end of the century allowed Remington, in the words of Rick Stewart, "to push the boundaries of bronze sculpture to their farthest limits and...challenge accepted ideas of mass, gravity, and motion in space"[11]; in pieces like *Coming Through the Rye* (plate 13), *The Mountain Man* (plate 12) and *The Cheyenne* (plate 4), Remington indeed created the "perfect expression of action"[12] he sought in sculpture.

By the turn of the century, Remington's art turned in new directions, partly because his "model" had undergone irrevocable changes—towns had overtaken the western landscape and settlers replaced rugged individualists. "The West," Remington declared, "is no longer the West of picturesque and stirring events."[13] As early as 1895, Impressionist influences appeared in Remington's oils; now, as Remington began using a broader, lighter palette and more careful brushwork, his figures became softer, his juxtaposition of man and nature more harmonious, and his landscapes shimmered with Impressionistic light and shadows.

As the Impressionist technique had freed the great French masters to capture a fleeting moment in time, it offered Remington the perfect way to preserve a world now fast disappearing. Royal Cortissoz commented on Remington's adaptation of Impressionism to the unique colors and images of his chosen subject, writing, "Under a burning sun he had worked out an Impressionism of his own...it is a grim if not actually blatant gamut of color with which he has to deal."[14] In pictures set in the evening or at night, Remington's play with light and shadow had startling effects: the flickering firelight in *Apache Medicine Song* (plate 22) renders the figures chilling and ominous, while the somber tones of *The*

Luckless Hunter (plate 20) endow the rider with a poignant and intense loneliness. Reviewing a show of Remington's oils in the Knoedler gallery in 1906, a critic noted the "extraordinary variation...of light flooding on canvas after canvas."[15]

Toward the end of his life, Remington reinstated the vigor of his early brushwork, wedding the Impressionistic with the realistic. *The Buffalo Runners* (plate 15), painted in the last year of his life, is a magnificent culmination of Remington's artistic development. Alive with the sunstruck colors of the prairie and painted in the bold strokes of Impressionism, it resonates with the spontaneous excitement of Remington's earliest sketches and watercolors. With this work, Remington achieved a long-held goal—to paint a "running horse so you could feel the details instead of seeing them."[16] In the sturdy bodies and determined faces of his riders, he created the ultimate image of the heroic westerner, one that endures as an integral part of American mythology.

Remington died in 1909. His legacy, as Theodore Roosevelt said in his eulogy, is clear: "The soldier, the cowboy and rancher, the Indian, the horse and cattle of the plains, will live in his pictures, I verily believe, for all time."[17]

NOTES

1. Peter R. Hassrick, *Frederic Remington: Paintings, Drawings, and Sculpture* (New York: Harrison House/Harry N. Abrams, Inc.,1987), 39
2. Ibid, 23
3. Ibid, 27-28
4. Rick Stewart, *Frederic Remington: Masterpieces from the Amon Carter Museum* (Fort Worth: Amon Carter Museum, 1992), 12
5. Ibid, 10
6. Hassrick, 33
7. Brian W. Dippie, *Remington and Russell: The Sid Richardson Collection* (Austin: University of Texas Press, 1983), 26
8. Stewart, 46
9. Dippie, 8
10. Hassrick, 37
11. Stewart, 43
12. Hassrick, 48
13. Dippie, 10
14. Hassrick, 47
15. Dippie, 46
16. Ibid, 52
17. Hassrick, 50

Amon Carter Museum

The Amon Carter Museum has one of the foremost collections of paintings, drawings, and sculpture by Frederic Remington and Charles M. Russell in the country, as well as major works by Georgia O' Keeffe, Thomas Eakins, Martin Johnson Heade, Thomas Cole, and Winslow Homer. Paintings, sculpture, and graphic arts of the nineteenth- and early twentieth-centuries are exhibited in a building designed by Philip Johnson, as are selections from the Museum's comprehensive collection of American photography.

Amon G. Carter, Sr., the Fort Worth publisher and philanthropist, discovered the work of Frederic Remington through his friendship with the writer and humorist Will Rogers. Beginning in 1935, Carter amassed a significant collection of the artist's work in order to establish a public museum devoted to American art. When the doors of the Amon Carter Museum opened in 1961, many of Remington's finest paintings and bronzes were displayed, as Carter had intended, as a testament to the pioneer spirit of the American West.

3501 Camp Bowie Boulevard
Fort Worth, Texas 76107
(817) 738-1933

Sid Richardson Collection of Western Art

The Sid Richardson Collection of Western Art displays a permanent collection of 55 paintings by Frederic Remington and Charles M. Russell. The majority of the works, reflecting both the art and reality of the American West, were acquired by oilman and philanthropist Sid W. Richardson from 1942 until his death in 1959. Richardson's love for western art grew out of his personal experience in ranching and his own impressions of the Old West. In Remington's and Russell's paintings he found much of the vitality and motion he always associated with his West.

Born in Athens, Texas, in 1891, Richardson attended Hardin-Simmons University in Abilene and Baylor University at Waco before entering the oil business at age twenty-two. Thereafter, oil, cattle, and land formed the basis of a career that paralleled the boom-and-bust nature of the petroleum industry in the 1920s and '30s. Since 1982, the Sid Richardson Collection of Western Art has been housed in an authentic replica of an original 1895 building, located in historic Sundance Square in downtown Fort Worth.

309 Main Street
Fort Worth, Texas 76102
(817) 332-6554